Hawker Tornado, Typhoon & Tempest
Janusz Światłoń

Introduction

The Hawker Typhoon and Tornado were British single-seat fighter aircraft designs of World War II for the Royal Air Force, intended as replacements for the Hawker Hurricane.

The Air Ministry advised Hawker that a specification was in preparation for a fighter using one of these engines to replace the Hurricane, and Hawker presented an early draft of their ideas in response. The requirement was released by the Ministry as Specification F.18/37 after further prompting from Hawker.

Two alternative projects were undertaken: the Type N (for Napier), with a Napier Sabre engine, and the Type R (for Rolls-Royce), equipped with a Rolls-Royce Vulture power-plant. Both engines had 24 cylinders and were designed to produce over 2,000 hp (1,491 kW); the difference between the two was primarily in the arrangement of the cylinders and crankshafts – a twin-crankshaft H-block in the case of the Sabre, and a single-crankshaft X-block in the Vulture.

Two prototypes of both the Type N and R were ordered on 3 March 1938. The planned production of Tornado was cancelled after the engine it was designed to use – the Rolls-Royce Vulture – proved unreliable in service. The parallel airframe for the Napier Sabre continued into production as the Typhoon.

The Hawker Typhoon was intended as a high- and medium-altitude interceptor, powered by the Sabre I engine. When this engine was finally available, it was soon discovered this model was difficult to start, engine sleeve jams caused the cylinder to explode, and it could cause dangerous amounts of carbon monoxide to enter the cockpit. The result was that the first development and production Typhoons were continuously plagued with technical problems related to the unreliable Sabre engine. Furthermore, mid-air structural failures of the joint between the forward and rear fuselage, and tail breakaways were experienced, caused by elevator mass balance assembly breakages and other faults. Flight testing continued into mid-1941 with a new prototype, the Typhoon Mk 1b, and despite its recurring problems, 1,000 aircraft were ordered for the RAF.

The Typhoon Mk 1b was fitted with the more reliable 2,180 hp Sabre IIA engine which enabled the fully loaded (13,250 pounds) aircraft to reach a speed of 412 mph, with a ceiling of 35,200 feet, and a range of 980 miles.

To support the D-Day invasion, the Royal Air Force formed the 2nd Tactical Air Force, which contained, among other aircraft, 18 squadrons of Hawker Typhoons. During the first five days of June 1944, the Typhoons put all but one of the Normandy coastal radar installations out of action. On D-Day itself, 6 June 1944, Typhoons continuously attacked the German armoured formation nearest to the invasion beaches, the 21st Panzer Division, which consequently suffered 26 destroyed or abandoned tanks.

During the four-month Normandy Campaign, 151 Typhoon pilots were killed, 36 were captured and 274 aircraft were lost to enemy action, mostly ground fire.

During the four years the Hawker Typhoon was in service, 670 pilots of its 23 squadrons were lost. By the war's end, 3,317 Hawker Typhoons had been built. By September 1945 the Hawker Tempest, which had gone into service in April 1944, had replaced the Typhoon Mk I. Unlike many other surplus fighter aircraft, such as Tempests, Hurricanes and Spitfires, which were sold to foreign air forces, all the Typhoons were scrapped within a short time of the war ending.

The Hawker Tempest was an improved derivative of the Hawker Typhoon, intended to address problems with the Typhoon's unexpectedly poor high-altitude performance by replacing its wing with a thinner design of a different profile.

In March 1940, engineers were assigned to investigate the new low drag laminar flow wing developed by NACA in the United States, and which was subsequently used in the new North American P-51 Mustang, with a symmetrical section and maximum thickness at 40% chord. Hawker designed a wing for the Tempest series which was a compromise between the new laminar flow sections and traditional profiles. It had a maximum thickness-to-chord ratio of 14.5% at the root (compared with 19% on the

Typhoon), tapering to 10% at the tip. The maximum thickness of the Tempest wing was set at 37.5% of the chord, compared with 30% for the Typhoon's wing.

The first Tempest prototype, Mk V HM595, was first flown by Philip Lucas from Langley on 2 September 1942. This aircraft retained the early Typhoon's framed canopy, car-style door, and was similarly powered by a Sabre II engine with a 'chin' radiator like that of the Typhoon. The Tempest was quickly fitted with the same bubble canopy fitted to Typhoons, and a modified tailfin that significantly increased the vertical tail surface area. The horizontal tailplanes and elevators were also increased in span and chord (and these surfaces were also fitted to late production Typhoons).

Even before the first flight of the prototype Tempest Mk V, a production order for 400 Tempests was placed by the Air Ministry. The order was split, with the initial batch of 100 being Tempest Mk Vs (retrospectively known as Series 1 aircraft), powered by the 2,235 hp (1,491 kW), Napier Sabre IIA series engine with chin radiator, while the with the Napier Sabre IV and wing leading-edge radiators. As it transpired, the difficulties with the Sabre IV meant that this version would never reach production and the order was switched to 300 Tempest Mk V Series 2s. The first production Tempest Mk V, JN729, was first flown by test pilot Bill Humble on 21 June 1943.

The Tempest Mk V was in the hands of operational squadrons by April 1944, with 3 Squadron the first to be fully equipped.

Tempests scored a number of kills against the new German jets, including the Messerschmitt Me 262. Hubert Lange, a Me 262 pilot, said: "the Messerschmitt Me 262's most dangerous opponent was the British Hawker Tempest — extremely fast at low altitudes, highly-manoeuvrable and heavily armed."

In air-to-air combat, the Tempest units achieved an estimated air combat success ratio of 7:1, accomplishing a 6:1 ratio against single-seat enemy fighters.

Variants

- Typhoon Mk II: The original designation of the Hawker Tempest.
- Tempest Mk I: Prototype fitted with the Napier Sabre IV engine with oil coolers and radiators placed in the wing to reduce drag, one aircraft.
- Tempest Mk III: Projected variant fitted with Rolls-Royce Griffon IIB. Not built (Mk III prototype serial LA610 transferred to a Fury prototype).
- Tempest Mk IV: Projected variant fitted with Rolls-Royce Griffon 61 engine. Prototype LA614 cancelled.
- Tempest Mk V: Single-seat fighter, fighter-bomber aircraft, powered by the Napier Sabre II engine, 801 built by Hawker at Langley.
  o Early series Tempest Mk V: The first 100 production aircraft were fitted with four long-barrel 20 mm (.79 in) Mk II Hispano cannon and utilised some Typhoon components.
  o Mid- to late-series Tempest Mk V: 701 production aircraft fitted with four short-barrel 20 mm Mk V Hispano cannon and other production line changes.
  o Tempest TT Mk 5: After the Second World War a number of Tempest Mk Vs were converted into target tugs.
- Tempest F Mk II: Single-seat fighter aircraft for the RAF, powered by a Bristol Centaurus radial engine, 402 built by Hawker at Langley and 50 by Bristol Aeroplane Company at the Banwell factory.
- Tempest FB Mk II: Single-seat fighter-bomber with underwing pylons for bombs and rockets.
- Tempest F Mk VI: Single-seat fighter aircraft for the RAF powered by the Sabre Mk V (2,340 hp) with chin radiator and wing-root oil cooler, 142 built.

Hawker Tornado P5219, the first prototype.
Lengley airfield, 6 October 1939.
Temperate Land Scheme camouflage pattern of Dark Green and Dark Earth upper surfaces with Night port wing, white starboard wing, aluminum front fuselage and tailplane. Serials and spinner black.

Hawker Tornado P5224, the second prototype.

Temperate Land Scheme camouflage pattern of Dark Green and Dark Earth upper surfaces with yellow under surfaces. Serials and spinner black.

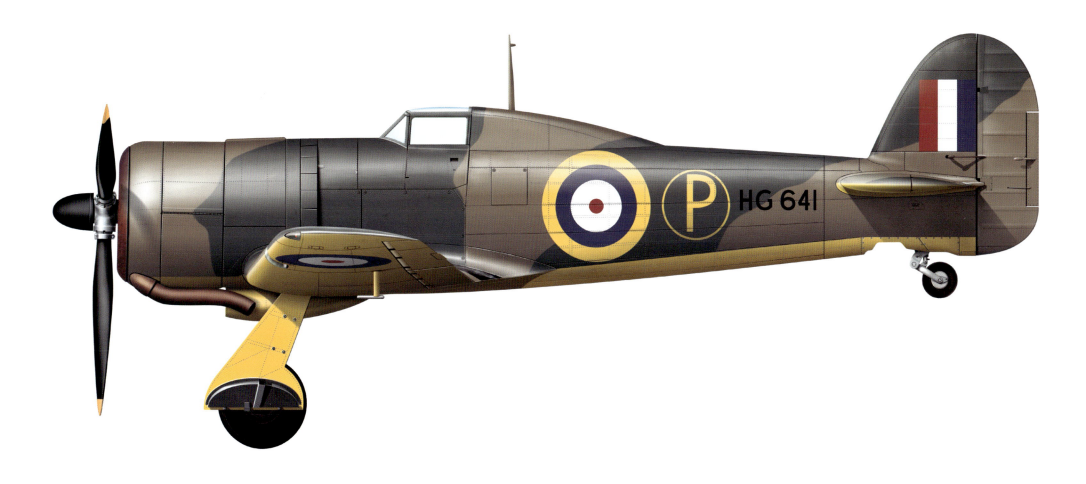

Hawker Tornado HG641, third prototype.

Aircraft with Bristol Centaurus CE.23, October 1943.

Temperate Land camouflage scheme of Dark Green and Dark Earth upper surfaces with Yellow under surfaces. Black serials, prototype symbol Yellow.

R7936

Hawker Tornado Mk Ia R7936 – production aircraft.
Aircraft with Rolls-Royce Vulture II engine and contra-rotating propeller. Woodford, 21 August 1943.
Day Fighter Camouflage of Dark Green and Ocean Grey upper surfaces with Medium Sea Grey under surfaces. Black serials.

Hawker Typhoon Mk Ia R7548 US•A "Farkquhar IV" of 56 Squadron RAF.
Duxford, UK, September 1941.

Day Fighter Camouflage of Dark Green and Ocean Grey upper surfaces with Medium Sea Grey under surfaces. Black serials.
Sky code letters, spinner and rear fuselage band. Rank pennant on the engine cowling. Aircraft name in white.

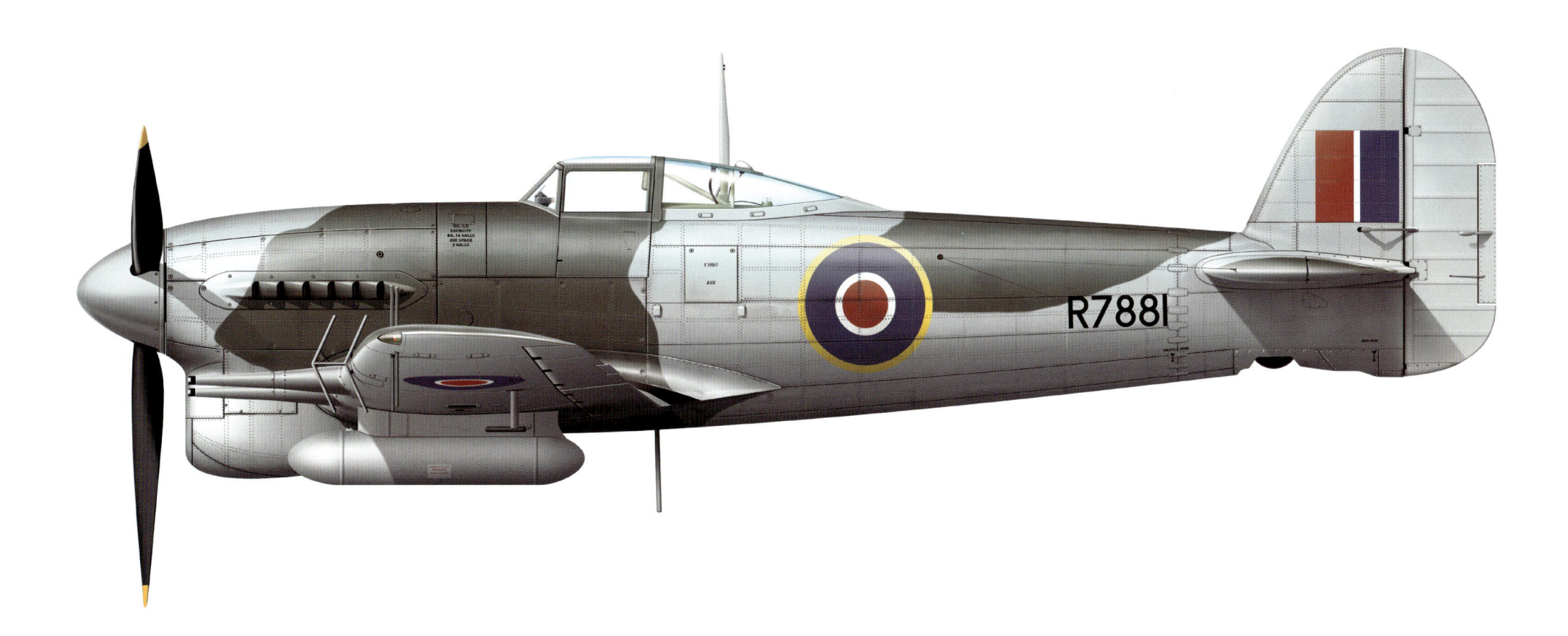

Hawker Typhoon Mk Ia R7881 X of 56 Squadron, Duxford, UK, 1941.
3-blade propeller, car door canopy.
Day Fighter Camouflage of Dark Green and Ocean Grey upper surfaces with Medium Sea Grey under surfaces. Sky code letters, spinner and black serials.

Hawker Typhoon Mk Ib DN323 Y• of 451 Squadron RAAF.
Egypt, April 1942.
Desert Camouflage scheme, Dark Earth and Mid Stone upper surfaces with Azure Blue under surfaces. Black serial and white code letter.

Hawker Typhoon Mk Ib MN134 SF•S of 137 Squadron RAF.
Personal aircraft of Flight Officer A.N. Sames, Manston, UK. June 1944.
4-blade propeller and bubble top canopy. Day Fighter Camouflage of Dark Green and Ocean Grey upper surfaces with Medium Sea Grey under surfaces. Black serials.
Sky code letters spinner and rear fuselage band. Individual letter repeated on the fin. Aircraft with full D-Day invasion stripes.

Hawker Typhoon Mk Ib EK139 HH•N "Dirty Dora" of 175 Squadron RAF.
Spring 1943.

Day Fighter Camouflage of Dark Green and Ocean Grey upper surfaces with Medium Sea Grey under surfaces. Black serials.

Sky code letters, spinner and rear fuselage band. Individual emblem in front of the canopy. Underwing special Identification Stripes, four 12 inch black bands and three 18 inch white bands. Carried by Typhoons from Dec 1942 to Feb 1945.

Hawker Typhoon Mk Ib MN353 HH•U of 175 Squadron RAF.
July 1944.

Day Fighter Camouflage of Dark Green and Ocean Grey upper surfaces with Medium Sea Grey under surfaces. Black serials and spinner. Sky code letters and rear fuselage band. D-Day invasion stripes only on the lower part of the fuselage and wings under surfaces.

Hawker Typhoon Mk Ib MN526 TP•V of 198 Squadron RAF.
B.10, Plumetot aviation base, July 1944.

Day Fighter Camouflage of Dark Green and Ocean Grey upper surfaces with Medium Sea Grey under surfaces. Black serials and red spinner. Sky code letters and rear fuselage band. Individual letter repeated on the fin and squadron code repeated on the fuselage cowling. D-Day invasion stripes only on the lower part of the fuselage and wings under surfaces.

Hawker Typhoon Mk Ib MP149 I8•P "Pulverizer II" of 440 Squadron RCAF.
Personal aircraft of F/O H. J. Hardy. B.78, Eindhoven., July 1944.
Day Fighter Camouflage of Dark Green and Ocean Grey upper surfaces with Medium Sea Grey under surfaces. Black serials and spinner. Sky code letters and rear fuselage band. D-Day invasion stripes only on the lower part of the fuselage and wings under surfaces. Individual markings painted on the engine cowling.

Hawker Typhoon Mk Ib R

B.10 Plumetot Ai

r Camouflage of Dark Green and Ocean Grey upper surfaces with Medium Sea Grey under surfaces. Sky code letters, spinr

DN 500
PSC G-5/169288
D.S.I

PSC G-5/17101 D.S.I

DN 500

R

Hawker Typhoon Mk Ib R7698 Z•Z "Penny" of "Duxford" Wing.

Duxford, UK, September 1942. Personal aircraft of Wing Commander Dennis E. Gilliam.

Day Fighter Camouflage of Dark Green and Ocean Grey upper surfaces with Medium Sea Grey under surfaces. Sky code letters, spinner and rear fuselage band.
Individual name painted in yellow on the cockpit door.

Hawker Typhoon Mk Ib R8224 "Land Girl" of 609 Squadron RAF.

White nose and spinner was an addition to the Tiffie ID white stripes tested by 609 Squadron after some aircraft were mistakenly downed by friendlies and was meant for head on identification by friendly aircraft. Day Fighter Camouflage of Dark Green and Ocean Grey upper surfaces with Medium Sea Grey under surfaces. Sky code letters, and rear fuselage band. Individual emblem painted in front of the canopy, starboard side. Underwing special Identification Stripes, four 12 inch black bands and three 18 inch white bands. Carried by Typhoons from Dec 1942 to Feb 1945.

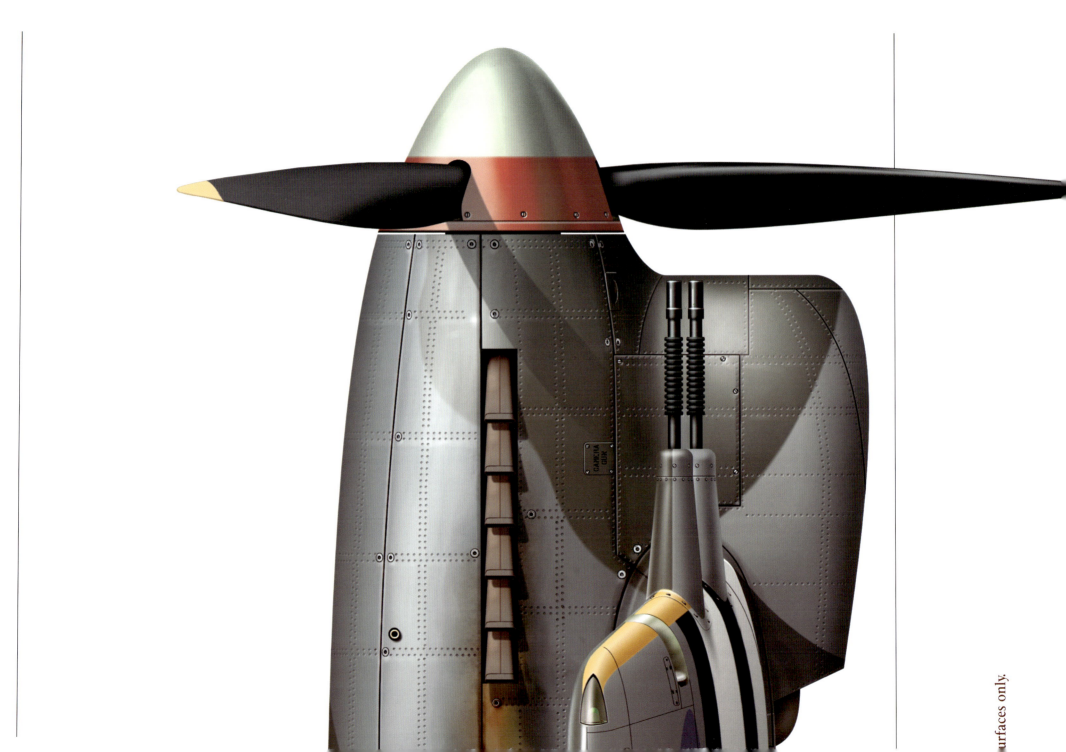

PR•D of 609 Squadron RAF.
, France, July 1944.

red band) and rear fuselage band. Individual emblem painted in front of the canopy. D-Day invasion stripes, wings under s

Hawker Typhoon Mk Ib R8639 FM•B of 257 Squadron RAF.
Usually flown by Flight Officer Cedric Henman, Exeter, UK, April 1943.
Day Fighter Camouflage of Dark Green and Ocean Grey upper surfaces with Medium Sea Grey under surfaces. Sky code letters, spinner and rear fuselage band. Individual emblem painted in front of the canopy, starboard side. Underwing special Identification Stripes, four 12 inch black bands and three 18 inch white bands. Carried by Typhoons from Dec 1942 to Feb 1945.

Hawker Typhoon Mk Ib MN882 TP•E of 198 Squadron RAF.
Summer 1944.

Day Fighter Camouflage of Dark Green and Ocean Grey upper surfaces with Medium Sea Grey under surfaces. Black serials and red spinner. Sky code letters and rear fuselage band. Code letters repeated on the fin. D-Day invasion stripes only on the lower part of the fuselage and wings under surfaces.

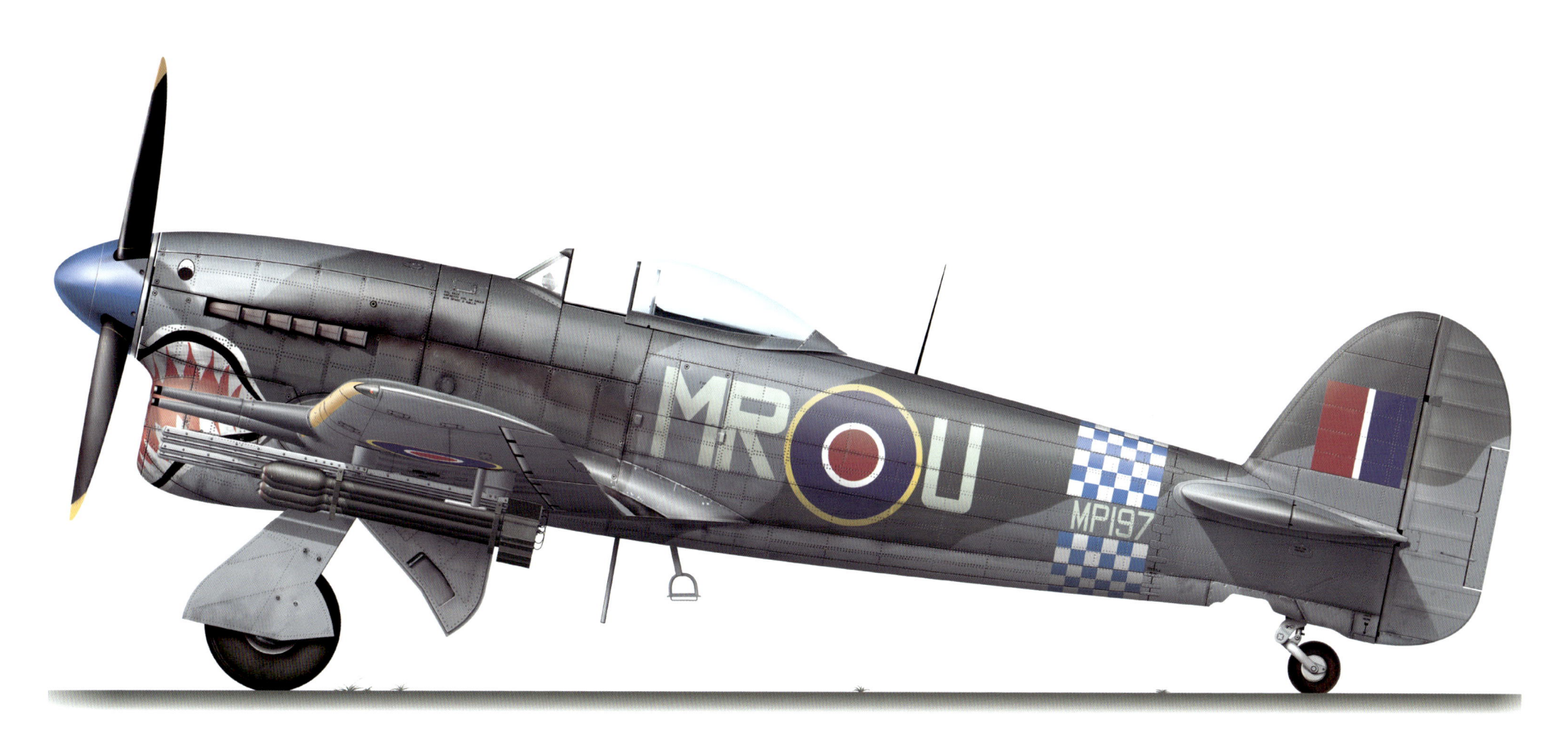

Hawker Typhoon Mk Ib MP197 MR•U of 145 Squadron RAF, BAFO.
Personal aircraft of Squadron Leader Anthony Zweigbergk, Germany, late 1945.
Day Fighter Camouflage of Dark Green and Ocean Grey upper surfaces with Medium Sea Grey under surfaces. Blue spinner. Sky code letters and serials.
Rear fuselage band in squadron colours. Shark mouth painted on the radiator scoop.

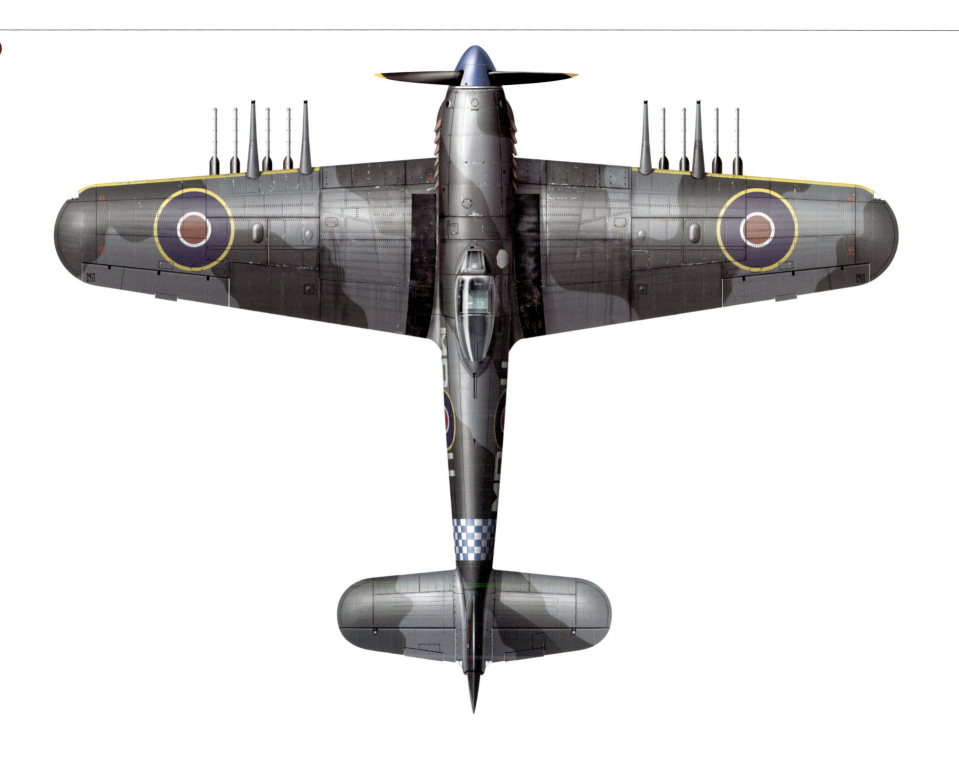

Hawker Typhoon Mk Ib MP197 MR•U of 145 Squadron RAF, BAFO.
Personal aircraft of Squadron Leader Anthony Zweigbergk, Germany, late 1945.
Day Fighter Camouflage of Dark Green and Ocean Grey upper surfaces with Medium Sea Grey under surfaces. Blue spinner. Sky code letters and serials.
Rear fuselage band in squadron colours. Shark mouth painted on the radiator scoop.

Hawker Typhoon Mk Ib R8893 XM•M of 182 Squadron RAF.

Day Fighter Camouflage of Dark Green and Ocean Grey upper surfaces with Medium Sea Grey under surfaces. Sky code letters, and rear fuselage band.

This aircraft carries the very short-lived white nose and spinner designed as a quick identification marking (Nov 1942), soon replaced by the black & white underwing stripes. This aircraft briefly wore both markings!

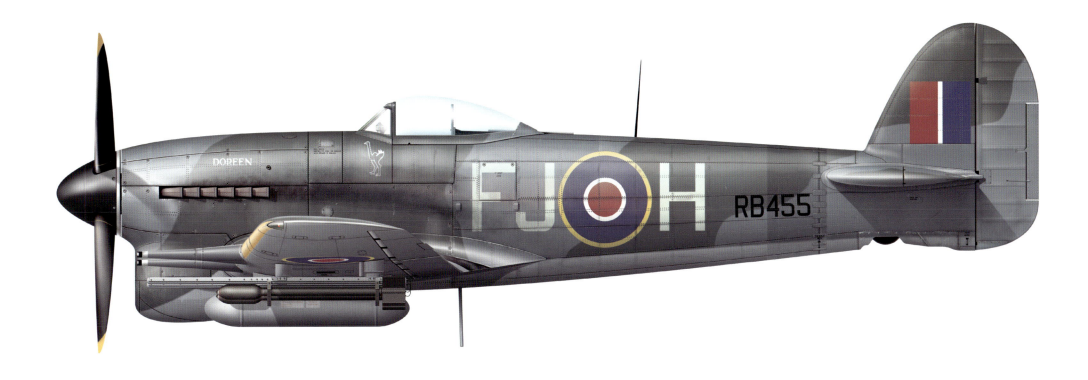

Hawker Typhoon Mk Ib RB455 FJ•H of 164 Squadron, June 1945.

4-blade propeller and Tempest-type tailplane. Day Fighter Camouflage of Dark Green and Ocean Grey upper surfaces with Medium Sea Grey under surfaces. Sky code letters, black spinner and serials. White personal emblem and name.

Hawker Typhoon Mk Ib SW493 DP•S "Betty" of 193 Squadron, 1945.
Aircraft was usually flown by S/L D.M. Taylor DFC.
4-blade propeller and Tempest-type tailplane. Day Fighter Camouflage of Dark Green and Ocean Grey upper surfaces with Medium Sea Grey under surfaces.
Sky code letters, black spinner and serials. White personal name on the engine cowling.

Hawker Typhoon Mk Ib T9+GK (ex EJ956 of 175 Squadron RAF).

Aircraft force-landed close to Marigny, France on 14 February 1944 flown by F/O B.F. Proddow.

Aircraft was repainted by Germans. Dunkelgrun and another colour uppersurafces. Tail and under surfaces in Gelb.

German code letters in white and black, also repeated on the wing under surface.

Hawker Typhoon Mk Ib MN454 HF-S "Diane IV" of 183 Squadron, late 1944.
3-blade propeller, Tempest tail plane, bubble canopy.
Day Fighter Camouflage of Dark Green and Ocean Grey upper surfaces with Medium Sea Grey under surfaces. Sky code letters, spinner and fuselage band. Black serials. Aircraft name painted in white on the engine cowling.

Hawker Typhoon Mk Ib RB207 F3•T "TESS" of 438 Squadron, 1945.
3-blade propeller, Tempest tail plane, bubble canopy.
Day Fighter Camouflage of Dark Green and Ocean Grey upper surfaces with Medium Sea Grey under surfaces. Sky code letters. Black serials and spinner.
Aircraft name painted in white on the engine cowling.

Hawker Typhoon TT Mk I SW500 12 of 56 OTU, 1946.

Day Fighter Camouflage of Dark Green and Ocean Grey upper surfaces with Yellow/Black under surfaces. Sky code letters, spinner and black serials.

Hawker Tempest Mk V prototype HM595.
Originally a converted Typhoon with old-style canopy and tail unit.
Day Fighter Camouflage of Dark Green and Occan Grey upper surfaces with Yellow under surfaces. Prototype symbol Yellow.

Hawker Tempest Mk I prototype HM599.

Day Fighter Camouflage of Dark Green and Ocean Grey upper surfaces with Yellow under surfaces. Prototype symbol Yellow.

Hawker Tempest Mk V prototype HM595.
Aircraft in its final configuration with additional dorsal fillet.

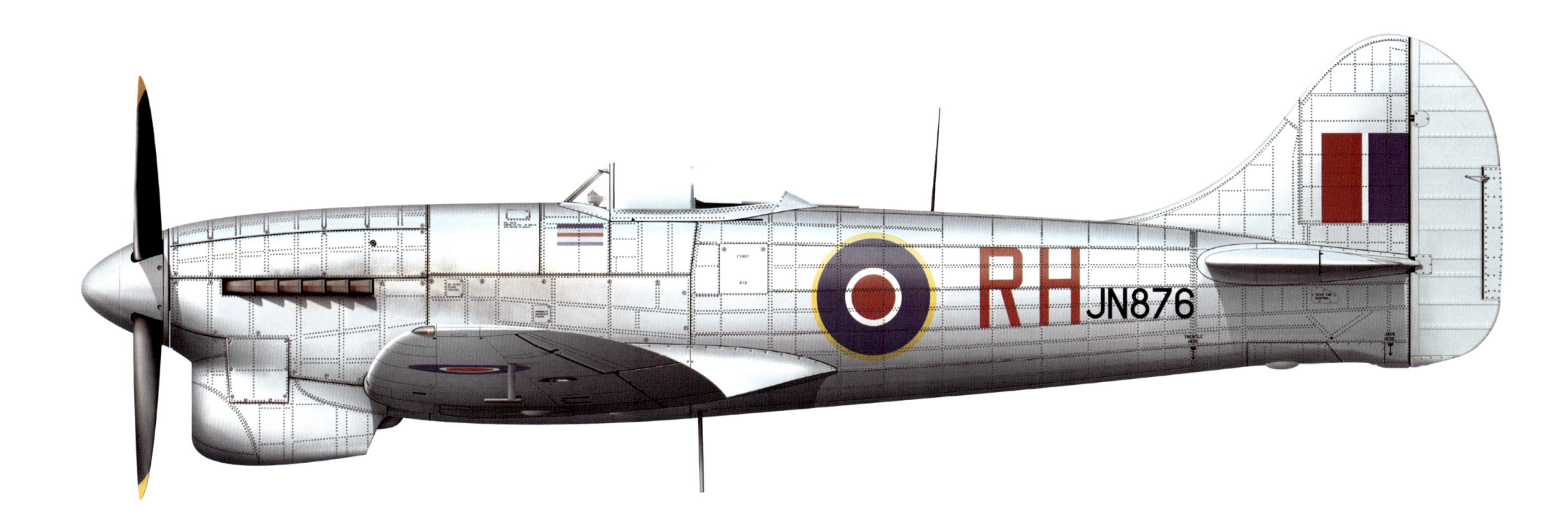

Hawker Tempest Mk V JN876 RH, 1947.

Personal aircraft of the Air Marshal Sir Roderick Maxwell Hill, Commander-in-Chief of Fighter Command.

Aircraft overall aluminum finish. Black serials, red code letters.

Hawker Tempest Mk V SN330 J5•H of 3 Squadron RAF.
Personal aircraft of Squadron Leader C.H. Macfie, Wunsdorf, Germany, 1947–48.
Aircraft overall aluminum finish. Black serials, green code letters and spinner.

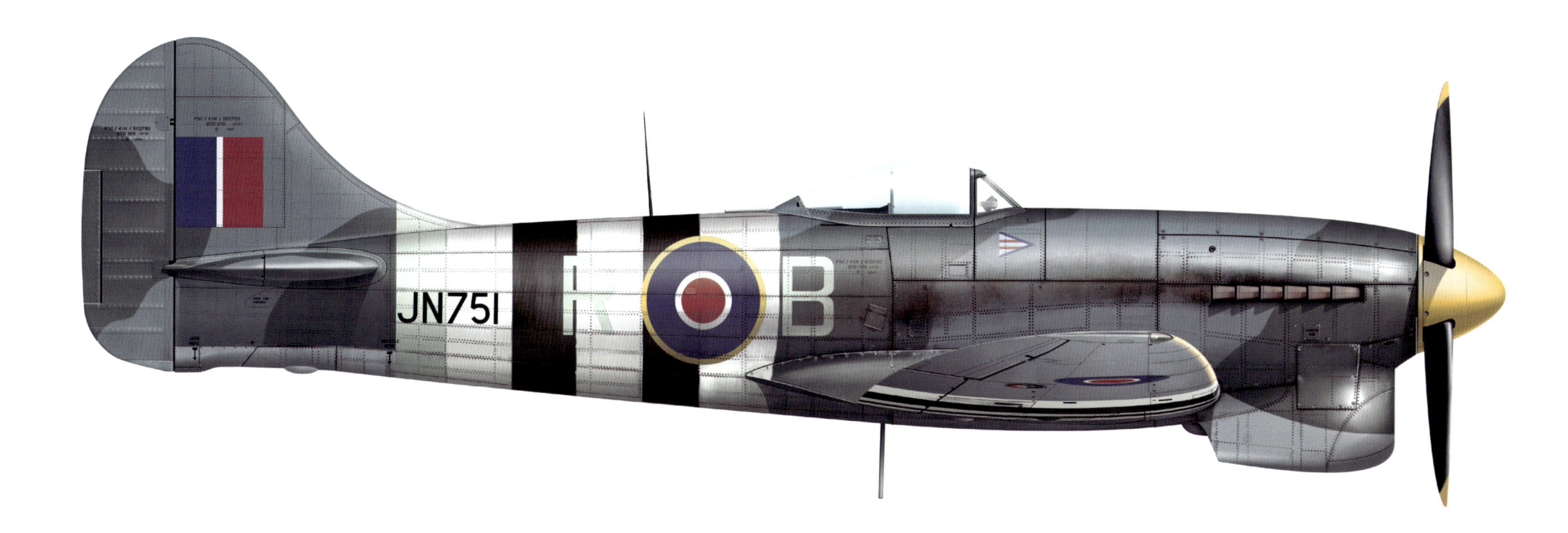

Hawker Tempest Mk V JN751 R•B of 150 Wing RAF.

Personal aircraft of Wing Commander Roland Prosper "Bee" Beamont, June 1944.

Day Fighter Camouflage of Dark Green and Ocean Grey upper surfaces with Medium Sea Grey under surfaces. Sky code letters and fuselage band. Black serial, Yellow spinner. Aircraft with full D-Day invasion stripes and rank pennant.

Hawker Tempest Mk V EJ533 SD•R of 501 Squadron RAF.
Manston, Kent, UK, 1944.
Aircraft overall aluminum finish. Black serials, code letters and spinner.

Hawker Tempest Mk V JN862 JF•Z of 3 Squadron RAF.
Personal aircraft of Flight Lieutenant R. van Lierde, Newchurch, June 1944.
Day Fighter Camouflage of Dark Green and Ocean Grey upper surfaces with Medium Sea Grey under surfaces. Sky code letters, fuselage band and spinner.
Black serial. Aircraft with full D-Day invasion stripes.

Hawker Tempest Mk V JN862 JF•Z of 3 Squadron RAF.
Personal aircraft of Flight Lieutenant R. van Lierde, Newchurch, June 1944.

Hawker Tempest Mk V NV768 with Napier Sabre VI engine and ducted spinner during test.

Day Fighter Camouflage of Dark Green and Ocean Grey upper surfaces with Medium Sea Grey under surfaces. Prototype symbol Yellow. Serials in Black.

Hawker Tempest Mk V NV724 JF•E "Le Grand Charles" of 3 Squadron RAF.
Personal aircraft of Squadron Leader Pierre Closterman, Volkel, Netherlands, April 1945.
Day Fighter Camouflage of Dark Green and Ocean Grey upper surfaces with Medium Sea Grey under surfaces. Sky code letters. No fuselage band. Spinner Red.
Black serial. Aircraft name and cross in white. Victory markings black and white.

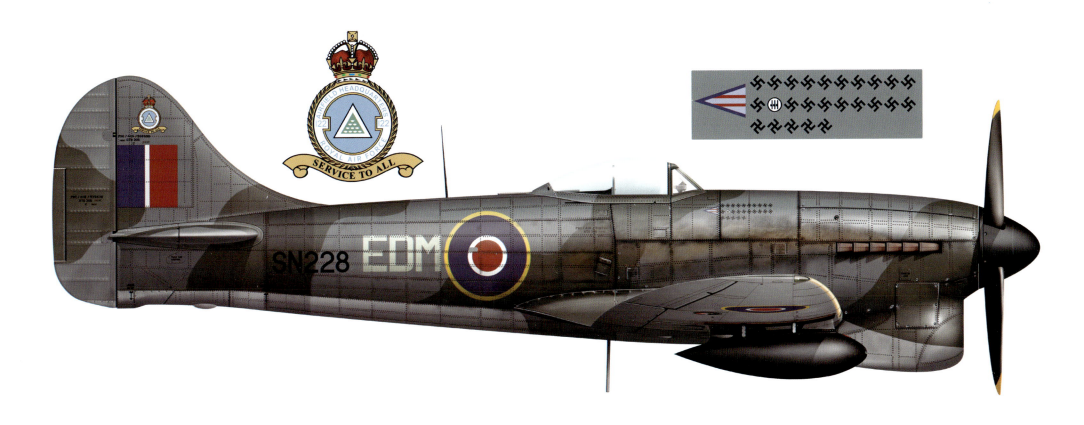

Hawker Tempest Mk V SN228 EDM• of 122 Wing RAF.

Day Fighter Camouflage of Dark Green and Ocean Grey upper surfaces with Medium Sea Grey under surfaces. Sky code letter. Black serial and spinner.
Victory markings black and white. Rank pennant below the canopy. Wing badge on the fin.

Hawker Tempest Mk V SN228 5R•S of 33 Squadron RAF.
RAF Base Gatow airfield, Berlin, Germany, 1946.
Aircraft overall aluminum finish. Black serials, code letters. Yellow spinner, fuselage stripe and canopy frame. 33 Squadron badge on the fin.

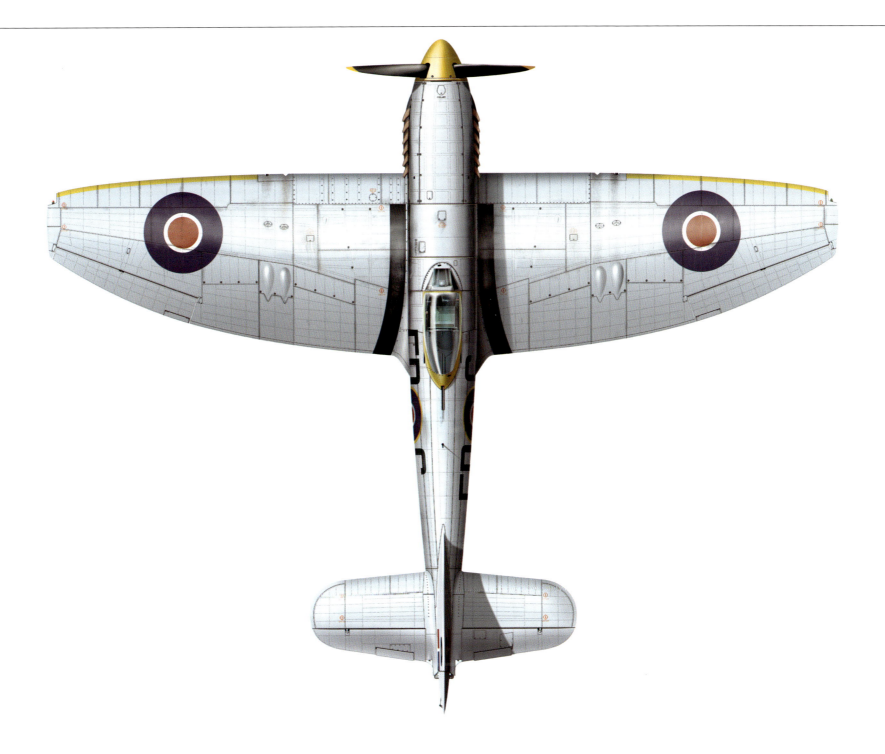

Hawker Tempest Mk V SN228 5R•S of 33 Squadron RAF.
RAF Base Gatow airfield, Berlin, Germany, 1946.

Hawker Tempest Mk V SN254 US•T of 56 Squadron RAF.

Day Fighter Camouflage of Dark Green and Ocean Grey upper surfaces with Medium Sea Grey under surfaces. Sky code letter. Black spinner.

Post War markings, including underwing serials in black. Rank pennant below the canopy. Squadron badge on the fin.

Published in Poland in 2016
by STRATUS s.c.
Po. Box 123,
27-600 Sandomierz 1, Poland
e-mail: office@mmpbooks.biz
for
Mushroom Model Publications,
3 Gloucester Close,
Petersfield,
Hampshire GU32 3AX
e-mail: rogerw@mmpbooks.biz

ISBN 978-83-8365281-09-8

Editor in chief
Roger Wallsgrove

Editorial Team
Bartłomiej Belcarz
Robert Pęczkowski
Artur Juszczak

Colour profiles
Janusz Światłoń

DTP
Artur Juszczak

Printed by
Drukarnia Diecezjalna,
ul. Żeromskiego 4,
27-600 Sandomierz
www.wds.pl
marketing@wds.pl

PRINTED IN POLAND

Also in this series.

Albatros Fighter Aircraft of WW1
DAVE DOUGLASS

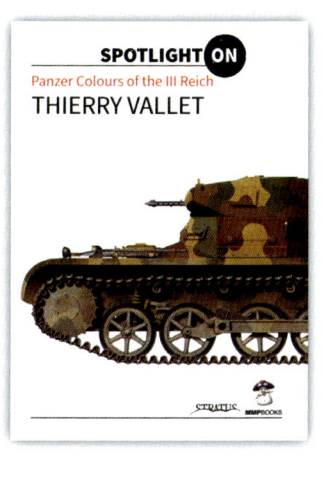

Panzer Colours of the III Reich
THIERRY VALLET

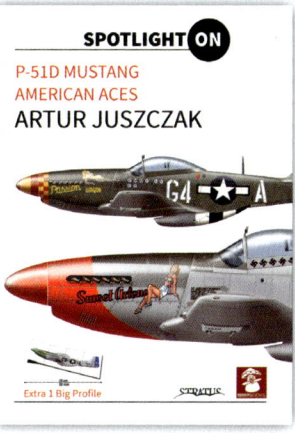

P-51D MUSTANG
AMERICAN ACES
ARTUR JUSZCZAK

Extra 1 Big Profile

Supermarine Spitfire V
ROBERT GRUDZIEŃ

Extra 1 Big Profile

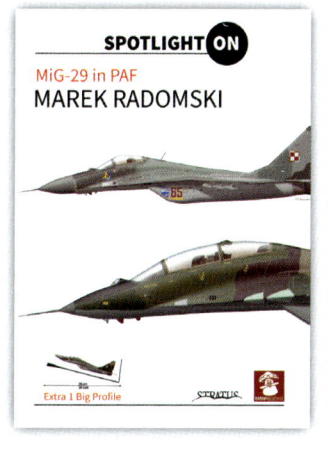

MiG-29 in PAF
MAREK RADOMSKI

Extra 1 Big Profile

Messerschmitt Bf 109 in Romania
**TEODOR LIVIU MOROȘANU
DAN MELINTE**

Junkers Ju 87 Stuka
SIMON SCHATZ

F4U Corsair
ZBIGNIEW KOLACHA